I0503566

Cryptocurrency Demystified

Everything you need to know about Cryptocurrency

Justin Harrison

FOREWORD

After the Bitcoin boom in 2017, most people have heard about Cryptocurrency. But strange enough, very few people actually know what it is and how it works.

Cryptocurrency and blockchain technology are here to stay so it's vital that you understand it - especially if you want to buy some in the future.

In this book, Justin takes an extremely technical subject and simplifies it. He shows you what Cryptocurrency and blockchain technology is in the simplest format that anyone can understand.

He goes through the pros and cons of cryptocurrency which gives you great insight into the reasons why mass adoption hasn't taken place yet and what it will take for it to become mainstream.

Finally, he discusses his approach to choosing cryptocurrencies which is brilliant and at the same time, simple and logical!

Justin applies logical thinking and old school investing principals to his cryptocurrency investing strategy, which I believe sets his advice apart from the others out there.

This will be your ultimate guide to understanding cryptocurrency and it will prepare you for the digital cryptocurrency revolution which is extremely exciting.

Well done Justin for taking such a complex subject and simplifying it the way you did.

David Bester

TABLE OF CONTENTS

INTRODUCTION

The internet has revolutionized the way we work and the way we communicate. It has changed the very fabric of our society by breaking down borders and making the world more accessible even in the most remote corners of our world.

Yet in stark contrast, money and finance have despite all the technological advancements in banking, remained under the central control of governments, unchanged since the inception of money itself.

In a world where we can skype call across the globe in an instant, transfer large digital files across oceans of fibre optic undersea cable in mere milliseconds, and all for free, doing a simple interbank transfer to your neighbour across the street can take days and cost you a small fortune, why is this the case?

The answer is government control. Governments want and need to control the flow of money in order to exist, in order to maintain their power structures. Without the control of money no government would have any control over its citizens.

Money to governments is an invisible prison for its citizens, they get to dictate how, when and where people can spend, move and save their money. Most often this is referred to as "foreign exchange control", which is nothing more than a smokescreen for economic oppression and imprisonment.

Cryptocurrencies have been created to challenge those power structures, to decentralize control and to place the power back in the hands of the people. But as with any early-stage innovation, these are murky waters, rife with misinformation from government sources and cowboy investors all looking to push their own agendas all looking to exploit people during these early stages.

Make no bones about it, cryptocurrency is here to stay. It's going to be a long road ahead before it becomes completely mainstream, accepted and understood by the majority of consumers on the ground, but mark my words when I say a revolution has started.

Young people are tired of centralized power structures, young people are indifferent to authority, and the future of cryptocurrency lies not in the hands of the generation that created it, but rather the next generation that will take it into the mainstream.

Steve Jobs and Bill Gates may have brought us the power of personal computers but it is the generation of Sergey Brin (Google) more notably Mark Zuckerberg (Facebook) that truly made the digital computer generation mainstream to an entire planet of people.

Cryptocurrency is at its infancy still and is challenging how we think of money and understand how commerce works but in the not too distant future everyone will understand Cryptocurrency in the same way we understand all other digital tools today.

In this book, I am going to take you by the hand and demystify Cryptocurrency for you so that you can become not only an early adopter but put yourself inline to be part of one of the single largest shifts in modern history.

For those who get it, there is a fortune to be made. Let's get started.

THE STORY OF BITCOIN

Bitcoin was invented in 2008 by an unknown person using the name Satoshi Nakamoto and started in 2009 when its source code was released as open-source software.

No one knows who Satoshi Nakamoto is. It could be a man, a woman or even a group of people. Satoshi Nakamoto only ever spoke on crypto forums and through emails.

October 31, 2008

Satoshi Nakamoto writes to a mailing list of an encryption site claiming to have invented an electronic currency that can finally create a monetary system without the need for a third-party trust (financial institutions), and also solving the problem of double-spending. In the email, the anonymous creator attaches a white paper entitled "Bitcoin: A Peer-to-Peer Electronic Cash System" in which he technically describes how Bitcoin works.

January 3, 2009

The source code of Bitcoin is released along with the first 50 bitcoins. The genesis block is undermined, within which a message is left with the title of the Times of the same day "Chancellor on Brink of Second Bailout for Bank", a phrase aimed at criticizing the current financial system that was about to collapse and needed a government bailout.

17 August 2010

Mt. Gox" was established, the first Exchange in which Bitcoin could be traded with normal Fiat currency. On the first trading day, the price of Bitcoin is $0.07.

10 February 2011

Bitcoin reaches parity with the US dollar for the first time, trading at 1 to 1.

2 April 2013

Bitcoin for the first time exceeds $100 dollars.

28 November 2013

Bitcoin for the first time exceeds $1,000 dollars to 1

bitcoin mark.

Bitcoin crisis

Between 2013 and 2014 several events cause the price of the bitcoin to collapse from the historical highs, leading many analysts to claim a premature end of the Internet currency.

Silk Road: the online drug marketplace is closed

In October 2013, Ross Ulbricht, the founder of Silk Road, the leading online drug and arms market in which the bitcoins had become the currency of choice, is arrested. This leads the press to link the two themes, presenting Bitcoin as a "drug currency", and the currency suffered a severe reputation set-back.

China prohibits the exchange of bitcoins

In December 2013, the Chinese central bank issued a warning to all financial institutions, companies and individuals, stating that any trade with bitcoin will then be considered illegal. Ironically at the time, 80% of the Bitcoin transactions were carried out within the People's Republic of China. In addition, on January 19 of the following year, Alibaba (the Chinese version of Amazon) cancelled bitcoin prices from its e-commerce portal, causing the virtual currency to lose its main world market.

Collapse of Mt.Gox

In February 2014, the world's largest bitcoin exchange, Mt. Gox is declared bankrupt after suffering a hacker attack, during which 850 thousand Bitcoins disappeared. Confidence fell drastically, bringing the price to lose 80% from the highs reached in the previous year.

Bitcoin reaches new highs

In 2015, institutional investors became increasingly interested in the technology that underpins Bitcoin, the Blockchain, which causes the price of bitcoin to once again exceed the psychological threshold of $1,000 per unit.

Along with a drastic rise in prices in 2017, media attention grows as does the fear of some governments that bitcoin could be used in a number of illegal activities, however, despite this, the price of Bitcoin continues to soar.

Buy the end of August 2017 there is a fork of the

Blockchain of Bitcoin that leads to the birth of Bitcoin Cash, which is identical to Bitcoin except for some differences in the size of the blocks and in the mining process.

Today

The rest, as they say, is history. The attention of venture capitalists on startups that use Blockchain technology, the attention of the media, the birth of new cryptocurrencies and the possibility of raising capital through ICO, have allowed Bitcoin to reach the value of $19,783 USD in December 2017. Far from those highs today, rest assured that a new peak is coming for Bitcoin in the future.

WHAT IS A CRYPTOCURRENCY

In non-technical terms, a Cryptocurrency is an internet-based medium of exchange which is better thought of as a digital or electronic currency.

Some people would also refer to it as a virtual currency, however, this is technically not correct. Virtual currency, for example, would be something more along the lines of voyager miles or in-game credits which would be limited to a singular marketplace, whereas digital currency is exactly like normal money and is widely accepted and can be exchanged between other currencies.

The most important feature of a cryptocurrency is that it is not controlled by any central authority, and this makes cryptocurrencies theoretically immune to the old ways of government control and interference.

Cryptocurrencies can be sent directly between two parties via the use of private and public keys. These transfers can be done with minimal processing fees, allowing users to avoid the steep fees charged by traditional financial institutions.

In more technical terms, a cryptocurrency is a digital currency that uses cryptography for security, making it very difficult to counterfeit, and because most cryptocurrencies are decentralized systems based on blockchain technology, with a distributed ledger enforced by a disparate network of computers, Cryptocurrencies provide users with transparency, and uneditable transaction history.

There are currently more than 1600 Cryptocurrencies, with some of the better-known ones being: Bitcoin, Ripple, Litecoin, PeerCoin, Dash, Steller, and Ethereum.

WHAT IS THE BLOCKCHAIN

At a normal bank, transaction data is stored inside the bank. Bank staff makes sure that no invalid transactions are made. This is called verification. Let's use an example;

George owes 10 USD to both Mark and John. Unfortunately, George only has 10 USD in his account. He decides to try to send 10 USD to Mark and 10 USD to John at the same time, however, the bank's staff notice that George is trying to send money that he doesn't have, so they stop the transaction from happening. The bank stopped George from double-spending which is basically fraud.

Banks spend millions of dollars to stop double-spending from happening, whereas Cryptocurrency makes use of Blockchain technology to verify all transactions and to keep a record of all transactions.

Blockchain technology is the backbone of any cryptocurrency. Blockchains hold the ever-growing permanent records of all cryptocurrency activity.

Each cryptocurrency's blockchain has all information about past transactions, addresses, wallet balances, and more; from the beginning (i.e. genesis block) to the most recent.

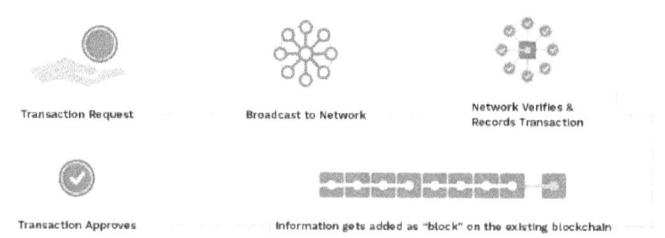

Transaction Request | Broadcast to Network | Network Verifies & Records Transaction

Transaction Approves | Information gets added as "block" on the existing blockchain

All cryptocurrencies use distributed ledger technology (DLT) to remove third parties from their systems. DLTs are shared databases where transaction information is recorded. The DLT that most cryptocurrencies use is called blockchain technology.

A blockchain is a database of every transaction that has ever happened using a particular cryptocurrency. Groups of information called blocks are added to the database one by one and form a very long list. So, a blockchain is a linear chain of blocks!

Once information is added to the blockchain, it can't be deleted or changed. It stays on the blockchain forever and everyone can see it.

The whole database is stored on a network of thousands of computers called nodes. New information can only be added to the blockchain if more than half of the nodes agree that it is valid and correct. This is called consensus. The idea of consensus is one of the big differences between cryptocurrency and normal banking.

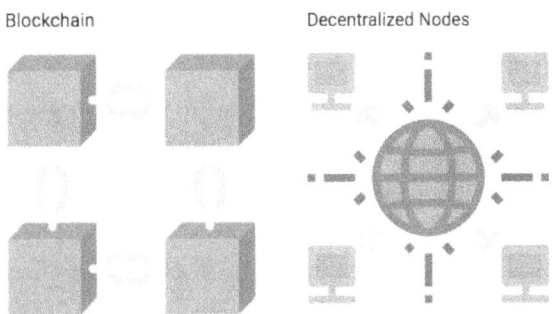

Blockchain   Decentralized Nodes

WHAT IS CRYPTOCURRENCY MINING

Mining is the process of validating other people's transactions with a computer and then adding them to the long, public list of all transactions known as the blockchain. In exchange, people get rewarded with cryptocurrency.

Anyone with a computer and an internet connection can become a miner. But before you get excited, it's worth noting that mining is not always profitable. Depending on several factors, such as which cryptocurrency you're mining, how fast your computer is, and the cost of electricity in your area, you may end up spending more than you earn back.

Cryptocurrency mining is one of the most commonly used methods of validating transactions that have been executed over a blockchain network. Not only does blockchain work to protect transaction data through encryption, as well as store this data in a decentralized manner so as to keep a single entity from gaining control of a network, but also the primary goal is to ensure that the same crypto token isn't spent twice.

In effect, "mining" is one means of making sure that cryptocurrency transactions are accurate and true, such that they can never be compromised in the future.

Cryptocurrency mining itself refers to a type of validation model known as "proof-of-work" (PoW). There are two common validation types, and we'll look at the other, known as proof-of-stake (PoS), in a moment.

The PoW model:

In the PoW model, which bitcoin, Ethereum, Bitcoin Cash, and Litecoin use, to name a few, individuals, groups, or businesses compete with one another with high-powered computers to be the first to solve complex mathematical equations that are essentially part of the encryption mechanism. These equations correspond to a group of transactions, which is known as a block.

The first individual, group, or business that solves these transactions, and in the process validates the accuracy of these transactions within a block, receives a "block reward." A block reward is paid out as digital tokens of the currency that's being validated.

As an example, the current block reward for bitcoin is 12.5 tokens. That means whoever is the first to correctly solve equations for a block is paid 12.5 tokens. Assuming the average price of bitcoin around $9,500 per coin, that works out to a nearly $119,000 haul.

Disadvantages to the PoW model:

There are two major concerns attached to the PoW model. First, it's an extremely electricity-intensive practice. To mine virtual currencies, massive mining centres with graphics processing units and/or application-specific integrated circuit chips (ASIC) are set up to handle this validation and processing.

The electricity costs, depending on where an operation is located, can be enormous. It could also, in theory, be a drain on local or national electric grids, depending on how large the digital networks and mining farms become.

The other issue is that the PoW model has a security vulnerability, at least for smaller digital currencies. Any individual or group that can gain control of 51% of a networks computing power could essentially hold that network and digital currency hostage. Networks the size of bitcoin, Ethereum, and Litecoin have next to nothing to worry about. However, newly issued coins with fewer participants could be susceptible.

Though cryptocurrency mining might often be lumped in as one big free-for-all, there are differences in the equipment being used to validate transactions. For bitcoin, miners need to use highly specialized and expensive ASIC chips because of the difficulty in validating bitcoin transactions. Meanwhile, most other virtual currencies allow miners to use some variation of graphics processing units from the likes of NVIDIA or Advanced Micro Devices to proof transactions. However, the difficulty in this mining can still vary from one cryptocurrency to the next.

The PoS model:

Even though there are technically a number of proofing alternatives, the biggest competitor to the PoW model is the proof-of-stake (PoS) model. With PoS, there are no high-powered computers and mining farms sucking up electricity to validate transactions.

Instead, stakeholders of a digital currency receive the randomized right to validate transactions. In plainer terms, the more of a cryptocurrency that you own, the more likely it is that you'll be chosen to validate a block of transactions. Those who are chosen don't receive a "block reward" when complete. Instead, they receive the aggregate fees from the transactions that were proofed.

The obvious advantage of this platform is that it's considerably lower cost. There's also no worry that hackers will gain control of 51% of a network's computing power with the PoS model. For hackers to gain control of a PoS-backed network, they'd need to control 51% of all outstanding virtual coins, which could get quite expensive.

Disadvantages to the PoS model:

Arguably the biggest issue with the PoS model is that major stakeholders can have a much larger say in the future path of a digital network. Whereas PoW networks are massive and incorporate the opinions of a lot of people, PoS networks lose some of the decentralization that makes cryptocurrencies special, therefore allowing larger players to shape future technical and economic pathways for a cryptocurrency.

It's tough to say which method developers will prefer in the years to come, but at least when someone talks about "cryptocurrency mining" in the future, you'll know exactly what they mean.

HOW DOES CRYPTOCURRENCY WORK?

C ryptocurrency is roughly the equivalent of using PayPal or a Debit Card, except that the numbers on the screen represent cryptocurrency instead of a FIAT currency like the dollar.

All a new user needs to do is set up a Crypto market account like Coinbase. there are many others such as Coinmama, CEX, Kraken, and Coinsutra to name a few. With Coinbase as an example, users can buy, sell, send, receive, and store Bitcoin, Bitcoin Cash, Ether, and Litecoin and other cryptocurrencies. Coinbase provides an all-in-one wallet, broker, and exchange service making them a one-stop-shop for new users.

To use cryptocurrency, you don't need to understand it (any more than you need to understand the monetary system to use a debit card). Cryptocurrency works a lot like bank credit on a debit card. In both cases, a complex system that issues currency and records transactions and balances works behind the scenes to allow people to send and receive currency electronically. Likewise, just like with banking, online platforms can be used to manage accounts and move balances.

The main difference between cryptocurrency and bank credit is that instead of banks and governments issuing the currency and keeping ledgers, an algorithm does.

Transactions are sent between peers using software called "cryptocurrency wallets." The person creating the transaction uses the wallet software to transfer balances from one account (AKA a public address) to another.

To transfer funds, knowledge of a password (AKA a private key) associated with the account is needed. Transactions made between peers are encrypted and then broadcast to the cryptocurrency's network and queued up to be added to the public ledger.

Transactions are then recorded on the public ledger via a process called "mining"). All users of a given cryptocurrency have access to the ledger if they choose to access it, for example by downloading and running a copy of the software called a "full node" wallet (as opposed to holding their coins in a third party wallet like Coinbase).

The transaction amounts are public, but who

sent the transaction is encrypted (transactions are pseudo-anonymous). Each transaction leads back to a unique set of keys. Whoever owns a set of keys, owns the amount of cryptocurrency associated with those keys (just like whoever owns a bank account owns the money in it).

Many transactions are added to a ledger at once. These "blocks" of transactions are added sequentially by miners. That is why the ledger and the technology behind it are called "blockchain." It is a "chain" of "blocks" of transactions.

Cryptocurrency can be obtained most of the same ways other types of currencies can. You can exchange goods and services for cryptocurrency, you can trade FIAT currency (i.e dollars) for cryptocurrencies, or you can trade cryptocurrencies for other cryptocurrencies.

Trading is generally done via brokers and exchanges. Brokers are third parties that buy/sell cryptocurrency, exchanges are like online stock exchanges for cryptocurrency. One can also trade cryptocurrencies directly between peers. Peer-to-peer exchanges can be mediated by a third party, or not.

Please be aware that cryptocurrency prices tend to be volatile. You should ease into cryptocurrency investing and trading and be ready to lose everything you put in (especially if you invest in or trade alternative coins with lower market caps).

To summarize:

- Cryptocurrency can be thought of as a digital currency like PayPal.

- Transactions and balances are recorded on a public ledger called a blockchain.

- Cryptocurrencies can be accessed through software called wallets (transactions are broadcast to the network to be added to the blockchain via transactions created in wallets). This can be equated to online banking (where you have account numbers and passwords and move funds between accounts).

- Cryptocurrencies can be bought through a broker or traded on online cryptocurrency exchanges (like a stock exchange).

- There are many other cryptocurrencies beyond Bitcoin.

- Unlike bank credit, which represents a centrally controlled and issued FIAT currency (like the US dollar), cryptocurrency is decentralized and thus not centrally controlled

- Instead of a central powering controlling cryptocurrency, an algorithm and users themselves control cryptocurrency. The algorithm dictates how transactions work and how new coins are created, users create peer-to-peer transactions using software called wallets.

- Those who confirm transactions by breaking cryptographic codes are called miners.

Of course, you don't need to know any of these key facts to use cryptocurrency. All you need to do is set up a Coinbase account and use that to buy and sell and to send and receive cryptocurrency, but hopefully, this will provide some understanding of how it works.

CRYPTOCURRENCY PRO'S AND CON'S

L ots of advocates of Cryptocurrency will tell you that it is the best financial system ever invented and that it has no faults. On the other hand, sceptics from the traditional world of finance will point to examples such as the illegal deep-web markets like Silk Road to try and convince you that it is just a tool for crime.

Techies love it, the DEA hates it, lawmakers are confused by it. So let's take a look at the pros and cons so you can form your own opinion based on facts.

Cryptocurrency Cons

- Secure and private transactions can lead to making it easier for people to skirt the law. Third parties involved in cryptocurrency, like those who produce wallets and exchanges, don't always have the same level of security as a coin's network itself.

- The value of cryptocurrency changes and laws on how to claim them as taxable income are fuzzy. It can be unclear as to how much value the coins have and thus can confuse what taxes should be paid on them. Should you pay based on what they were worth when you got them, or what they are worth when you file? There are answers to these tax questions, but it is complicated! Also, the private nature of transactions can make avoiding paying the proper taxes easy.

- Cryptocurrency is only accepted by certain vendors. Between that and fluctuating prices the money saved in transaction costs could be negligible.

- Cryptocurrency mining (at least in proof-of-work systems) is a CPU intensive process that requires an extraordinary amount of resources for no purpose beyond regulating coin creation and encryption.

- The cryptocurrency market is volatile, the value of coins can change wildly in a short amount of time. In 2014 the value of bitcoin ranged between about $30 and $1000!

- The coin you trade for a legal thing today can be used to fund awfully illegal things tomorrow.

The notorious Silk Road allowed for illegal black market transactions. While all currency runs this risk, cryptocurrency makes this easier to pull off.

- Not having a central bank control cryptocurrency adds to its volatility as no central force can step in to correct the markets (although this can differ by coin).

- If something goes wrong with a transaction or if a coin is lost there is no way to recover it. If someone does steal coins there is no way to rectify the issue.

- There is no way to recover coins if they are lost and there is no system in place to protect the value of your coin.

- Any given cryptocurrency lacks the flexibility of centralized currency due to its non-inflationary nature.

- Some privacy coins aside, cryptocurrency is not totally anonymous in most cases. The public ledger system might provide others insight into previously unknown economic activity.

- Cryptocurrency is software-based. Software, in general, can be hacked and have bugs, and blockchain-based networks have some theoretical vulnerabilities. Although Bitcoin's network has never been hacked, in large part due to its design, exchanges, wallet software, other cryptos, etc can be subject to hacks and bugs in practice and in theory.

Cryptocurrency Pros

- Most cryptocurrencies are built from the bottom up with security and privacy in mind. This means users can expect transactions to be private and secure despite non-identifying transaction data being public.

- Cryptocurrency is legal and, if it is claimed correctly for tax purposes, opens up another avenue for transactions.

- Cryptocurrency has low transaction costs compared to other digital payment methods like PayPal.

- Through the process of mining (securing cryptocurrency transactions), anyone with access to a computer and the internet can make money mining coins.

- Since the cryptocurrency market is volatile it

can be a high reward (albeit high risk) investment.

- Cryptocurrency makes trading anywhere in the
world easy. It's a decentralized currency. This
opens up financial options for people in countries that don't have access to financial services.

- Cryptocurrency is decentralized, meaning it
can't be deflated or inflated due to the choices of
a central government.

- Transactions are quick, permanent, and hard
to fake, this eliminates a lot of the fraud issues
banks deal with.

- There is no other entity that controls your
money or its value.

- Cryptocurrency isn't inflationary. With coins
like bitcoin, there is a set amount that will ever
be created.

- Cryptocurrency is transparent despite its
privacy features. This is called being pseudo-
anonymous. This transparency helps build security and trust and creates a level playing field.

- Cryptocurrency was designed from the bottom
up to be a secure system. In the history of Bitcoin, there has never been a successful hack of

the Bitcoin network. This can in part be attributed to Satoshi's focus on this problem from the get-go. For example, a major feature of the Bitcoin network is how the system prevents double-spend attacks.

There are lots of truly great things about Cryptocurrency. Believe it or not, the developers and designers of systems such as the Bitcoin network intentionally built properties into their systems that have made cryptocurrency a competitive alternative financial systems like the banks, and PayPal.

Currently, many banks and financial institutions don't serve poor, rural areas (especially in smaller countries). In 2011, the World Bank estimated that 64% of people living in developing countries lack access to basic financial services. Further, there are many people who are financially crippled by their governments' devalued currencies.

Cryptocurrency offers an alternative to the status quo that provides anyone with internet access with robust financial services. This is especially important for the impoverished and oppressed, as they often don't have a viable alternative.

THE FUTURE OF CRYPTOCURRENCIES

Today, though there are over a thousand cryptocurrencies, mostly taking Bitcoin's original source code and tweaking it. Yet, only a handful are accepted by retailers as a method of payment. The top three on the list are Bitcoins, Litecoins, and Peercoins, these being considered the more "stable" of the cryptocurrencies.

Unsurprisingly, fluctuations in the price of the Bitcoin generally drive faith in all the other cryptos. Since its launch in 2009, the price of the Bitcoin has climbed from less than a $1 to over $19,000. Recently, holding cryptocurrencies as a speculative asset rather than an actual currency per se has become far more attractive to the financially savvy.

With no government or "anchor" backing up cryptocurrencies, the only foundation that cryptocurrencies have is people's faith in their value. In other words, solely the market mechanism determines the price of cryptocurrencies.

The unprecedented rise in popularity of cryptocurrencies has caused legislation to lag, and people have to date taken advantage of this. Whether it is trading cryptos on an exchange, performing arbitrage, buying drugs online, or even something as simple as moving money across borders to avoid the many administrative and transactional costs involved. The rise in popularity in cryptocurrencies is very much driven by sheer need.

Some of the limitations that cryptocurrencies presently face are that one's digital fortune can be erased by a computer crash, or that a virtual vault may be ransacked by a hacker, which may be overcome in time through technological advances. What will be harder to surmount is the basic paradox that bedevils cryptocurrencies in that the more popular they become, the more regulation and government scrutiny they are likely to attract, which erodes the fundamental premise for their existence.

While the number of merchants who accept cryptocurrencies has steadily increased, they are still very much in the minority. For cryptocurrencies to become more widely used, they have to first gain widespread acceptance among consumers.

However, their relative complexity compared to conventional currencies will likely deter most people in the immediate future, except for the technologically adept and the early adopters who want to be in on the new wave.

That being said, as consumers become more educated, as systems become simpler and retailers and businesses begin to adopt crypto as a form of payment, the market will eventually follow suit.

There are already talks about major cryptocurrencies being listed on various stock exchanges, and banks are already looking at ways to integrate with cryptocurrencies which will further fuel the cryptocurrency revolution.

Whilst cryptocurrencies remain highly speculative now, and frankly, there are just too many cryptocurrencies in the market at present eventually a few will win out. Consumers and businesses of all sizes will see the advantages.

Afterall long before the rise of cryptocurrencies we had already entered the age of digital currency when we started using internet banking, debit cards and credit cards, the only difference with cryptocurrencies is that there is a fundamental shift in power away from the banks and governments into the hands of the people, and that is a good thing.

CRYPTOCURRENCY TRADING

G reed is a horrible thing, it's a horrible, horrible thing! Like it or not we all have this little bug in our system called FOMO (fear of missing out) and that little bug coupled with our natural greed is the cause of a lot of unnecessary pain and suffering.

Hopefully, this chapter will give some logic to your greed and bring about some calm to your FOMO, because without it if you jump into crypto trading you are are going to lose more than your shirt.

To begin with, you need to accept and understand that traditional currency trading, that being FIAT currency like the dollar, euro, pound etc is highly speculative to begin with and those are already established currencies. So when it comes to crypto trading no matter what any expert tells you, it is a pure gamble at best.

Now I know I have been talking about cryptocurrency being a real contender in the future and I have even gone as far as to say this is the future of money, however, what nobody can predict is which currency and what format it will be in.

Out of 1600 cryptocurrencies on the market today, most of them offering amazing systems and benefits there is no way in hell 20 years from now even 20% of them survive. This is like the dotcom boom and bust all over again, so we need to exercise a lot of logic and a whole bunch of caution.

If you are considering investing or trading in cryptocurrencies, it may be best to treat your "investment" in the same way you would treat any other highly speculative venture. In other words, recognize that you run the risk of losing most of your investment, if not all of it. If you cannot stomach that kind of volatility, best you look elsewhere for investments that are better suited to you.

HOW I CHOOSE MY CRYPTOCURRENCIES

I have been on the cutting edge of technology and more specifically financial technology since 1999. I spent my formative years in the heart of Silicon Valley during the dotcom boom and bust years, and I have outlived and outclassed my peers in the tech space despite being labelled as "old fashioned" and "conservative".

At a time when venture capitalists were throwing money at anyone with a good idea and a decent hair-cut, I chose to go the other way. I knuckled down, created amazing technology, grew companies from the inside out, built a loyal customer base and focused on making a profit by delivering exceptional service.

Why am I telling you this, and what does this have to do with cryptocurrencies? I am telling you this because I am "old fashioned" and "conservative". I have always maintained that the way people look at the tech space is entirely wrong.

You see the internet, technology, cryptocurrencies these are not new ways of doing business, these are simply alternative ways of delivery. For the most part, business stays the same, the rules don't change much, yet somehow people think they do.

To oversimplify, in the old days we took our product to market on foot and traded it for other product (called bartering), then we upgraded to the horse and carriage, built trading businesses and instead of bartering took money instead in the form of gold.

Eventually, that gave way to trucks and trailers and paper money, and today we have the internet and cryptocurrencies. This is the evolution of money, commerce and people.

But guess what, the basic rules of business have not changed for millennia, things like supply and demand, providing good service, trust, and ease of doing business. **So why then should the way we value an asset be any different?**

Before I answer that question, if you have not already read my book $MONEYSECRET which provides a very factual based history of money and why people are messing up properly when it comes to their personal finance, may I suggest you go get yourself a copy here

So back to the question, if we know that the basic rules of business apply no matter the vehicle of delivery, then why on earth should we value assets any differently than we always have? Yet that's exactly what people are doing every single day.

Imagine this for a second, if I presented an empty jar of air and asked you to place a value on it. You might say it would be worth X, someone else might say it would be worth Y. The reason for this is that the air inside the jar is essentially intangible and therefore the value is highly subjective and open to "opinion".

Now imagine if I presented the same jar filled with water and asked you to place a value on it. Chances are you would be far more likely to offer a realistic value. You would most likely look at the amount of water (weight, millilitres, the quality of the water, etc). The two items (air and water) are very similar, however, water is something we can touch and see, something we can "place value on".

And this is the secret to how I value cryptocurrencies, there has to be something tangible that underpins the value of the currency other than pure sentiment

There are basically only 3 tangible items that can underpin a cryptocurrency:

- A cap limit on the amount of currency in circulation.
- That the currency has a direct value underpinned a physical commodity.
- That the currency has a direct value underpinned an industry

Bitcoin, for example, has a cap on the amount of coin in circulation, there are only 21 million available. This means that there is a definite cap on the amount of currency in circulation, which means prices cannot be manipulated simply by adding more coins into the market.

Onegram and Karatcoin, for example, are underpinned by gold, meaning the value is directly linked to the amount of gold they hold in reserve and the fluctuating gold price, so this gives these kinds of cryptocurrencies a physical and intrinsic value.

Then there are currencies like Potcoin that underpin an industry. Potcoin was formed to solve the problem cannabis retailers were having in getting access to traditional credit card and merchant facilities despite the easing of drug laws around cannabis.

Potcoin has since become the sort of default industry currency, providing thousands of legitimate businesses with access to banking and payment facilities that would otherwise not have been accessible to them purely based on the financial industry's prejudice.

And it would also be worth mentioning a cryptocurrency like Ripple, who is in my opinion set to become what the US Dollar is to FIAT currency in the cryptocurrency space because the seem to be leading the pack in terms of becoming the default cryptocurrency to interchange with the banks and other FIAT currencies.

So my advice when you look to speculate in the cryptocurrency space, go old school and make sure something other than pure sentiment underpins the currency you are looking to invest into, with more than 1600 to choose from it will be an important benchmark.

CAN CRYPTOCURRENCY SAVE THE WORLD?

I often like to say that life is all about perception. Most people walk around mostly oblivious to the reality around them because perception is often stronger than reality.

If you have read my book $MONEYSECRET you will know that while currencies used to be backed by real assets. This was called "the gold standard", however, most currencies of today are not, and therefore subject to whatever value we place on them.

Ironically when advocates for the traditional financial system argue against cryptocurrencies they use the argument that nothing underpins the value of crypto currencies, which is hypocritical when you consider the facts.

You have to ask yourself, Is it a coincidence that an unknown programmer creates the most financially empowering object for humans the same year that global financial markets took a huge hit? Some might say "When a door closes, a window opens."

Whatever the case, governments around the world, most of which suffer from financial mismanagement and in some cases, outright corruption, have, in some cases, caused hyperinflation and subsequent suffering for their citizens, many of whom are simply trying to continue to live their lives. In these countries, the value of the fiat currency drops so quickly that by the time the worker takes their pay and attempts to use it to purchase goods, it has devalued to being completely worthless.

Citizens can empower themselves by moving to more stable currencies like Bitcoin or other cryptocurrencies (some of you may snicker, but compared to the steep drop in the value of something like Venezuelan currency, Bitcoins fluctuations are nothing) like "stablecoins" (a cryptocurrency pegged to real assets—like gold—or another fiat). Even those in the developed world can gain by moving to cryptocurrencies for transactions.

It's especially easy for the unbanked to do this, as cryptocurrency wallets can be created using a phone, with no more functionality than SMS. You don't need a telecom operator or any bank to be able to market and make useful a cryptocurrency on any mobile phone.

The decentralized ledger can be audited at any mo-

ment in time by its users, and you get the benefits of direct human-to-human transactions without
snooping or multiple fee-charging intermediaries.
Cryptocurrencies provide many benefits over fiat
currencies, and it's easy to see them as the currency
of the future.

As governments get more unstable and cash poor
and corporates violate personal data in search of
more data-driven business models to supplement
lost ad revenues, what better way to protect your
hard-earned money and information against all of
these interesting times than to leverage these currencies from the future?

When the internet was first envisioned, it had the
potential to become a medium which truly con-
nected any human on the planet to any other human
on the planet, without intermediaries. This technology can finally drive the internet to return to
those roots.

With cryptocurrencies, humans are free to transact
with each other, in a cash-like way, without cash.
And, cryptocurrencies just may save the world at the
same time by forcing governments to become more
accountable and for people to become more transparent with each other when doing business.

FINAL THOUGHTS

W hen the internet was first introduced it was slow and overly technical. It was inconceivable that just two decades later it would be so embedded in the fabric of our society that we can hardly function without it.

Such is the nature of chance, first, we resist it, then before we know that change is part of us, and I predict this is what will happen with cryptocurrencies.

I am however not advocating that you should be running out to buy crypto or moving all your payments in crypto over traditional currency. What I am suggesting is that you keep your finger on the pulse, that you speculate and hold onto some of the better-emerging cryptocurrencies, and that by doing so you put yourself in a position to take full advantage when the world does begin to swing more towards crypto.

These are exciting times, don't get left behind, but don't lose your shirt simply to have some skin in the game. It all comes back to logic.

ACKNOWLEDGEMENTS

I would like to thank my business partners, Dale Maxwell, Laura Palmeri, David Bester and Chris du Toit who have held down the fort while I took the time to write this book. Without their support and input, this book would never have become a reality.

I would especially like to thank Laura for her critical eye and constant proofreading, which helps a dyslexic, barely literate guy like myself seem capable of writing something worth reading.

I would also like to extend an extra-special thank you to my wife Andrea who as always offers constant constructive criticism and input, and unwavering support. Thank you for always making sure I have no distractions when I write and for your total commitment. I could not have asked for a better partner.

Last but not least, I would like to give an extra heartfelt thank you to David for sharing my vision and helping bring these ideas to life. Your work ethic and dedication to Global Money Academy is inspiring.

First printing, 2019.

Team 6 Investment Holdings Ltd.
5th Floor, Ritter House,
Wickhams Clay II,
Road Town, Tortola
British Virgin Islands

www.globalmoneyacademy.com